LAN S

DAVID NORRIS-KAY
&
WENDY WEBB

CW01082083

ISBN: 9798838276872

Words by David Norris-Kay & Wendy Webb ©2022
Front cover photograph "Burbage" David Norris-Kay ©2022
Front cover design CT Meek ©2022

David & Wendy have asserted their moral rights to be identified as the
Authors of this Work in accordance with the Copyright, Designs and
Patents Act 1988.

First edition published by Inherit The Earth Publications
©2022
In conjunction with Amazon.

Preface

David and Wendy agreed to write this book together with each submitting over 20 poems each. Rather than alternate their work we decided on dividing the book into two chapters, each containing their individual poems. While compiling this book I found their narratives distinctive, inspiring and highly intoxicating. Both authors express a heady brew of personal experiences and lyrical rhythms I found truly enchanting. You are entering into a magical realm of mesmerising poetry.

Meek

Editor

June

2022

Dedicated to all the poets and editors who've inspired me through the years.

David

June 2022

In memory of poets and friends, loved and lost, family and days gone

Wendy.

June 2022

David Norris-Kay.

Coggers Lane (*Hathersage*)

It rises
To pastoral paradise.
Clouds like white sheep
Dot the view.
A spill of fields flows
To the brush of cliff wood
And the frowning buttress
Of Carhead rocks
Shatters the sky.

Captivating panoramas
Shrink
The valley's steeple
To a miniature.
The Summer scent
Of trees
Evoke a renaissance
Of thoughts
From meadow stillness.

A ghost
Conjured from chimera
Rushes from remembrance
To blend present knowledge
With the boy I was:
Innocence and maturity
Metamorphose
Above the valley's echoes

(cont.)

Of church-bell chimes -
And years collide
In tatters of taunting time,
Tempestuous as life's
Brazen tears.
An aria of air
Sings through lofty leaves.
Now darkening the day,
Arboreal shadows
Fan over fallow fields.

Memories Of Hills

Haunting, cloudy through the mind,
Memories of a steep grass hill,
Ghostly in a purple evening:
Sun's dying shadow lingers still.

Distant folds rise to the stars,
No greater strength in shadowed sleep
Recalls the blackness of the groughs
Where tears of ice re-form and weep.

The gritstone's hard, it shapes the man
Who dares to tread on mountains mean:
Increases strength of mind and will
And sets a fast and certain scene.

Advancing dreamy mists of night
Brings coolant wine of lonely thought
And sound of phantom-sprayed cascades
Draws closer purposes long sought -

And when dawn streaks an Eastern sky,
The cumulus of wind-drawn day
Unfolds a rolling weathered moor
Of blending tinted seas of grey.

Memory fades illusions shades:
Leaves a river of sliding time,
Consuming thought and deed and life,
To bring in death, a higher climb.

A Daughter's Smile (*For Carol*)

Through hazy shades of dream you sense
The backward-teeming years of guile,
Which built a barrier of tears
In the transience of her smile.

Such years betrayed your love so much,
A sacred love you held awhile,
Much closer to your fragile days,
In the presence of her smile.

Now she prefers a life apart,
Her thoughts of you still infantile,
Yet hope will haunt cold emptiness'
With memories of her smile.

(*Published in 'Metverse Muse', India*)

Distance

I left her in the wild wood's thrash,
Where wind-rubbed branches percussion
Beat a tattoo through our distance.

Passion faltered in the year's grip:
Year upon year, love's force had slipped
Down the swirl of adversity -

Lost in a swamp-sink of boredom.
Mad-marching legions of routine
Had trampled first feelings to dust;

Ground us into the barren land
From which we had sprung: Tender green
Shoots on a hard city highway.

We are gratefully extinguished
By cold draughts of cruel logic
Howling from first fatal passion

Seated only in lust: I left
Her in the wood's tree-tortured murk,
Forlorn, and alone with our child.

Little Girls In Pink

Through the cracked paint of years
I seek their bliss,
In the sun-misted meadows
Of recurring dreams.

Little girls in pink,
Perfection of the Earth,
Skipping through the endless days
Of their slow sunrise.

They lure with soft innocence
And unassuming grace
Down the flower-tangled lanes
Of a land I have lost -

Which will be forbidden to them,
When their slender beauty fades:
Melting into womanhood,
And time's material cares.

(1982)

Self-Portrait
(*Pessimism is the seed of creativity*)

I am the mirror of my years,
Where shadows fall on ways unseen
By conscious sight: and all my pain
Reflects upon a face serene.

Time's beard has bushed a happy smile:
Slowed the fluttering wings of breath.
A string of days is drawing taut
To choke the joy of life with death.

From birth a path of dark and light,
Has wound towards this dizzy height,
Where now I stand, hold childhood's hand
And fall towards the falling night.

Lorraine, Aged 8

A perfection of childhood
I never attained,
Shines from your eyes
Like Elysian fields
Of endless Summer.

Weed trails gossamer-ice
Where you run and laugh,
Blonde and elusive
Across a gulf of years.

Soft face:
Fragment of sunshine,
Snares me in an aching
Exigency of love -

Clouds pale,

Feeling flows into voids
Like a liquid -

Drowning

Dissent that flares
On our borders.

I reach a hand...
To grasp your pure song
In the hidden dens of June:

(cont.)

My stain cannot taint
Your virtuous,
Visionary pools of light.

I become flotsam -
Born on a wave of blossom
As it crashes and dies
On my fading, adult shores.

Butterfly

There is no savagery or ruthless vice
In this unchained flower,
Dragon-flamed wings ignited
By the snaking-grasses fuse.

Mantras of war are for birds, beasts and men
To chant incessantly
Until they draw
Their last rattling battle-breath:

You rise from the killing-grounds
To celebrate the sun,
A nectar-primed power-pack
Crackling with the potency of flight:

Flashing over a tree-bordered twilight of water,
Born with the weed-seed
On singing sedge-combed breezes
Which stir the haystack's flaxen thatch:

You are an Aeolian ghost:
Brought on a wind of dreams from lost childhood,
Red admiral of blushing skies,
Haunting sorrel-sown spinneys of Summer:

Evoking from time-buried years,
A laughing, bright-eyed innocence, which drove
My agile body through swaying Wheatfield dawns
Dense with the kindling colours of quivering wings.

(cont.)

I caught you clinging to a bending poppy's plume,
Like a fragment of the setting sun,
Ephemeral as smoke, yet graceful in your dying,
Bowing out to the cloud-crinkled evening.

(*First Prize Winner in the Salopian Poetry Competition*)

(*Included in my collection,*
'From Time-Buried Years' Indigo Dreams Publishing)

Hide And Seek
(*For the daughter I never had*)

Above the 'hidden dens of June'*
Fresh fleshed trees wave;
Scratch against Summer's
Blue dome: I hide from fears,
Curl inside the sound
Of a green musical rustle.

You seek my breathless form
Lost in the wood's wavering winds
That stroke your soft hair
With a deeper softness.

I rise from fears; suddenly stand:
You shout, giggle, point,
Jump into my grasp
That trembles down the years
Into a mist of memory.

You were eight years old,
Rushing to the threshold
Of experience.

I, aged thirty –
Had drowned in it.

A line from David's poem 'Lorraine aged 8'

Autumn's Reflection

The cold astronomy of night
Imprints the Autumn chill
And in the gale a crying voice
Tells tales from overseas:
'The soldiers boots are clods of mud'
'And bayonets slash the moon'
'A starving child gropes for a hand
To guide him through the war'

And leaves in England drift like waves
From green and brown to gold,
Reflecting pain that memory hides
Within its prison walls,
And the government will always win
The losses of the world,
As a poor man fights with waning strength
To keep a wife and child.

Too many hearts of stone exist
In the morning of a dream,
And fail to sense outside themselves
The wide expanse of love.
As winter's shadow covers fields
In quiet lands of snow,
The beast of progress devastates
The root of all that's true,

And no-one ever will return,
To journey paths of sun,

(cont.)

Where a wasteland lies beneath the stars
Over which my words are flung.

Like empty caves in which the lies
Of nations echo through,
The hollow years destroy the smiles
Of those who breathe anew.

Included in his collection 'From Time-Buried Years (IDP)

Leam Farm

My youthful feet crept down the dusk-deep lane.
From the shelter of Sherriff wood's shadow –
I came across it, tranquil under hills,
Its chimney-wisp of smoke calmly climbing.

In frostbit fields, its mysterious barns
Awakened my teenage romantic dreams
Of living there, in chicken-clucking air
And the lowing cows' moody-morning breaths.

Now etched permanently in hope and mind,
It became an icon of my ambition
To work in those meadows, under new skies,
In the valley's bowl of shivering light.

Leaving these thoughts to unknown futures' grace,
The lane bore me west to face a red sky.
Sunken sun succumbed to indigo night,
And the first, hard pin-heads of lonely stars.

Dream Of Storm *(Cinquain Sequence)*

Fields lit
Through cloud-clearings
Patchworked with sun-touched gold:
Shadows move into their corners,
Tremble,

And reach:
Spread their dark tides
Between the corn's quiver
And yellow, pillared stalks. The crops
Waving.

Sighing
To changing skies.
The rain's cold ablutions
Bathe misty stacks of storm
That clash.

Lightning
Flickers the hills,
Forks fire into field ruts,
Briefly burns and purifies earth.
My thoughts

In awe
Of atmospheres,
Whose power overwhelms
Emotions of rising anger.

(cont.)

My tears
Raining
Sadnesses, blow -
Dispersing a foggy
Atmosphere of childhood gardens:
Quickly

Bringing
The black cloud's plumes
Out of my memory,
Into perspectives of peaceful
Lost years.

Eskdale

On choppy seas of low cloud,
Slate-peak islands
Float rain-blotted deeps:
Dark mammoth hill-heads
Obscure cold space,
Their strewn boulders
Jammed in jumbled symmetry:

Dislodged,
They would fall into alien worlds:
Deep valleys of men and time.

Absolute silence fine-tunes
To a perfect pitch of peace,
The black bell of night,
Its East rim gilded
By a cloud-feathered sun.

Dawn is an intruder,
Returning bleating life
To slate-slabbed dominions
Of scattered sheep.

*(Inspired by my love of the English Lake District,
and memories of climbing its hills in the 1960s)*

Bleaklow

(A high plateau in the Peak district)

Suspended beneath the stars,
Vague, without dimension
Dark moorlands sleep,
As vapour, like fingers
Touch and fill the hollows,
Blanketing the wasteland
In a white dream-shroud.

Unchanged by time's progression,
It makes apparent
My mortal weaknesses,
Like some alien petrified sea
Starkly grasping for the sky.

Dawn steals upon me from the East,
Slowly, without repercussion,
And, too aware of my frailties,
I stand, intruding the barren wilderness,
And witness the genetics
Of a perfect Pennine day.

Dark Earth

Dark earth which spawned
Young rose-blooms smooth,
When Spring's cologne
Heals bleeding hearts,
Conceal me in your fragrant folds,
For time seeks death
And joy it thwarts.

Dark earth the womb
And fetter of men,
Bring forth your bread
In ear of corn,
Where furrows cut
Through season's toll,
Come storm of night
And radiant morn.

Dark earth which holds
Loved friends in sleep,
While torments rage
On faith's keen blade,
Keep fast your deadly
Secret gates,
Till love's dug deep,
And lives are frayed.

(February 1971)

Lost Lad

Curtains of cloud drift apart
And shafts of sunlight spotlight a cairn,
Where Derwent and Howden moors meet
On hazy horizons of tors.

Succumbing to huge howling storms,
He scratched 'Lost Lad' onto a rock.
The final act before he froze
And ice welded him to the moor.

This height, a memorial now,
Forever named after his scrawl:
Where clouds shed tears of rhythmic rain
Above the reservoirs' domain.

*(Lost Lad - A hill in North Derbyshire where a young lad lost his
way and died of exposure)*

Dragonflies

Ghostly, omni-directional,
Stirring micro-paths
Twisting through Summer's
Fragrant Jungles of blossom:

Alighting weightless,
Spider-limbs quiver
Beneath a fragile form,
Reflecting morning glimmers
On hazy ponds
Of rippled light;

Delicate as sunshine:
Folding gossamer wings
Under drooping fronds of willow.

Young girl reclines
In dappled shadow,
Hears a soft fluting
Of wind-song, drifting
Through tall reeds,
Directed
At the delicate insect -

Flitting darkly past her slender legs,
Like some fairy of herself;
Illuminated briefly
By Heaven's

(cont.)

Golden fire.
Two Dragonflies
In a birdsong morning.

Ghosts

Silence and darkness
Pervade the trees,
Where mellifluous voices
Rang from echoes of dreams,
And barefoot children
Danced to their heartbeats
In the new-made warmth
Of untrammelled joy.

The years gather in
Ephemeral days –
That seemed would last
The life of the sun:
And young lives fade
In a sadness of loss,
Leaving beautiful ghosts
To our fears of old age.

(1982)

Beyond Realms Of Thought

My spinning, dream-drugged mind reveals
A far sun-cluster's galactic rim,
Revolving through a greater depth,
To where the starlight flickers dim.

Only human myth can suggest
A strangeness of endless spatial dark,
In margins beyond all realms of thought,
Where blind, distorted creatures walk.

Sliding through silent spheroid night,
Pass technological ships of man:
Ethereal, awful distances,
The power of life and death will span.

(Published in 'Bard 86' (Atlantean Publishing) and 'Star Tips For Writers' magazine)

In Dreams

When moonlight pales
The span of night,
Or mist's white cape
Diffuses sight;
Then colours fill an inner world
Where tapestries
Of dreams unfurl,
And endless deeps
Of sighing sea
Turn thoughts to dream
And comfort me,
But soon the leaves
Of memory fall:
They cover life's
Unclear recall,
Within the fantasies that wait
Through midnight's black
And starless gate,
Where shadows soothe
All selfish gain:
Some quench the sparks
Of mortal pain.
Then savage storms
Of nightmare rage;
Trap me within
Frail body's cage,
Inviting thoughts
Of turgid lust –
When uncontrolled
Destroying trust.
Soft-treading ways
Beyond the sun,
Where fevers fade,
Mistakes undone.

(cont.)

Our dreams can calm
All rising fear,
And when we wake
Will disappear.

Outcrop *(Two Tankas)*

Fields like starched white sheets
Below the gritstone's grey dream
Of cold crinkled clouds,
Invoke a shiver in me:
Conjures a cataclysm.

Rocks rock with wind's push:
Threaten to topple from high
Their great weight of stone,
Until calm comes quietly
As the snow. Halts disaster.

Lost Garden

The hay cart rots in clinging grass,
And rain slants through the day.
Old rusting wheels with hubs of brass
Sink in the sodden clay.

Here fading foxgloves sadly hang
On dehydrated stalks,
And under trees where blackbirds sang,
The ghost of childhood walks.

Now all is quiet, where I wheeled
My hay-cart over earth:
In silent supplication, kneeled –
To greet my brother's birth.

I knew not then he'd never shin
High oak trees in the lane,
Or he possessed beneath his skin,
An oxygen-starved brain.

Now he resides so far away,
And memories are gone
Of silver skies and hay-cart play,
When he was less than one.

He never knew the sway of trees,
Where feathered breezes blow,
Nor felt the numbing winter freeze
And gentle kiss of snow.

(cont.)

Instead he sat within his room,
And spent his early years,
Unheeding an impending gloom,
Concealed in falling tears.

Now in the garden chaos reigns:
Flowers and weeds entwine,
In protest at my brother's pains,
And indirectly mine.

The garden's lost inside my head:
Once close-razed lawns aren't mown.
The velvet foxgloves now are dead,
And all the birds have flown.

(For my youngest brother Robert, who has severe learning difficulties and now lives in local authority care)

(Winner of the reader's vote in Reach Poetry)

Exit *(Royal Hospital, Sheffield, 1970)*

The door to freedom is locked
With the key of pain.
Tissue-gnawing fear and uncertainty,
Like diver's ballast,
Weigh the body down
On a strange bed.
The human tide
Has washed him broken on a shore
Devoid of personality.
Only diseases exist here,
Neatly categorised and guarded
By strict doctrine.
His visitor's offerings
Of pantomime-smiles, are gestures
False as the doctor's
Whispered euphemisms.

Birds still sing in his dreams,
Where he walks whole and healthy,
Proud as Casanova,
Bearing his trophies
Of chastened girls:
A stirring of libido
Is extinguished by the smell of death,
In air that once rang
With the throaty birth-cries
Of his entrance.
The featureless ceiling
Which he knows better
Than his own wrinkled hands,
Reflects the pale light
Of a vanishing sun.

(3rd in Reach Poetry's Reader's vote)

Girl

Five years old:
You are the silky fruit
Of patient evolution.
Product of countless aeons,
Yet unaware of time's whorl,
Which, having created you -
Waits to destroy.

Your eyelids -
Fragile as innocence,
Flutter over pools
Of baby-blue beginnings,
Spangled with sparks of hope,
That dimly light your labyrinth
Of incipient, fearful life.

Dream while you can:
There is no Ariadne's thread
To lead you home.
Sad will be the day
When those eyelids open
In a wrinkled face
And see only oblivion.

Parting

The black of her coat
Is part of the night,
As she treads the path
From me to sole sleep,
Where in a warm dark
Of mythical depth,
An image of love
So softly will creep.

A scatter of stars
Reflect in my eyes,
As I face a world
Divided from yours,
And in lonesome realms
Engulfing our smiles,
The distant dim suns
Caress shapeless moors.

Summer Sunday

Receding thunder rumbles
Along ripples of grey
Dispersing cloud.
My dog
Snuffles the stillness
Of Stoke wood.

Above me
Sun-shinned boles
Burst into green
Rustling canopies,
Steaming in mist,
Streamed with Summer gold.

I return to The Rookery*,
Wading through gangling grasses:
Distant Wye resplendent
In smooth weirs
And a country-chorus of birds
Echoes through limpid light.

By the swimming pool's
Blue eye -
We take afternoon tea
Under pristine parasols,
And a rapture of recall.

(*The Rookery: A friend's house in the Peak District.)

35

Burbage *(Peak District Moors)*

Cooled lava slabs table the brown,
Where white cloud's fists clench in deep blue,
Their conspiracies of breezes.

Mix these mists in the darknesses
Which span me: Where thunderheads build
In high cradles of memory.

Where one slip could send me rolling
Down stone-strewn slopes: Into futures
Drowning in crippling pains of age.

Grey and black vapours consume me:
Fog the ambitions of my thought
Down a hidden warren of years.

Crows like a shoal of shadowed fish:
Frightened: Flap in my weathered wake,
Painting the bleak moonscape with life.

Now, brief hopes hover their bright ghosts
Through this wild land's echoing caves,
Blending Burbage with future dreams.

Sunshine Girl *(For Lisa)*

Shy face, corn-coloured sun-touched hair
Held in a space of time and light.
Never ageing in my gentle,
Recurring dreams, she's ten-years-old:
Now in a café or a park -
And always sunlight in her hair:
Always innocence and giggles
That lead me into happy night,
Holds me in dreamt nostalgia,
Until the dawn awakes my fears.

Four Cinquains

Dawn
>A great

Gap in grey cloud:

Red rays flow forth, reflect

From fenestrated twinkling towns

That gleam.

Day
>A cold

Blanket of light

Wraps frosty fields in fog,

That swirls in a swathing brightness
>And stays.

Dusk
>Soft mists

>Diffuse cloud-capped

>Mountains in lonely murk,

>And render the river's ripples
>So vague.

Night
>Darkness

>Spins silk-soft webs

>Where no spiders scamper

And spreads solid shadow in sparse
>Valleys.

*(First published in 'Muse Clad In Costumes' by Bernard M
Jackson and Dr H Tulsi. - India)*

In Memory Of Alan.

1954 – 1970

(Killed In A Motorcycle Crash)

Youth is laughter:
And you laughed
As I lay with my love
Among dim lights,
Enmeshed in the sounds
Of psychedelia.

You rode the saddle
Of a freedom that scorned girls,
Gauntlet-hands gripping steel,
Trailing highways of laughter
Through grey light:

Your bones lie severed
In an abstract of twisted chrome,
And still in quiet hours I hear
The laughter of your early death
Mocking my rejection by love,
And the awful
Rotting Winter of the years.

Wendy Webb.

Bembridge

The water flows like stainless steel, to pool
In ornate oval lily pond, in bloom.
Italianate, the gateway looking post
Attracts the able-bodied to its view.
Familiar formal bedding dances daydreams
Of cosmos/begonia/petunia/verbena.
Shady loveseat corners drip wisteria,
While tropicals/olive tree tubs grace
Picnic corner.
You want to know if this is to die for? No.
The solitary crow prays for his dinner.
Hums of biplane aches beyond the blue
And Lifeboat Station's closed, near the
Clifftop Café.
The tide is dredged to empty; vivid seas
Host sailing boats and ferries back and forth.
Night darkens late, for entertainment beckons,
With groan-worthy stomachs for feast and fortitude.
My husband brings pre-drinks and nibbles, hoping
Knees and hips will last the course until dark.

27 Today

I bought a ring today:
Sterling silver, cubic zirconia,
Patterning of wavy seas and sparkle.
Sat '*like a steam train*'
Of Bake & Grind '*at the station*'
Awaiting arrivals and departures
(of cupcake and mocha).
'*Steam erupts, spoons stir*'
As I remember 27 years – gone so fast.
'*But the journey's just begun*,'
Sat in Muffin Break in the shopping mall,
Placing the brand new ring
                              On my little finger;
Beside the green stone (almost 10).
So how would you celebrate?
Think I don't deserve it; should forget?

That mountain – 10 – sinks horizon in late-Fall;
beside a virgin ring on my little finger.
Pray for starry skies, dark passing clouds
to count stark shades tonight.

That I'm mum?
Numb. Mumbling. Mummers in a play…
'*Alas, poor Yorick! I knew him, Horatio.*'
Horatio? Andrew.
My boy: so loved, so wanted,
                        So worth remembering.
Raise a glass, anyone?

(cont.)

That date – 27 years ago –
We didn't bring baby home
                    To meet big brother.

Divine Journey

The journey is divine. What grows on trees
Is the cocoa pod, tended on family farms,
In Rainforests of West Africa, they tease,
'Please pick me when we're ripe. I'm bitter/sweet.'

From Mayan and Aztec pre-history they came,
A currency exchange that's so divine -
Noble Fests of chocolate were drunk
In Central Africa. Chocolate aimed to please.
So soon, it came to symbolise romantic love,
A luxury harem available to all,
From cocoa pods fermented in the sun,
Dried and shipped to factories worldwide.
Farmers driven to change; will chocolate cease
To bring delight to billions, so divine.
How to protect the Rainforest, reduce climate change?
Guardians of divine wisdom attempt Fairtrade,
So lovers may luxuriate and taste
Sweet or bitter potions of the great
alchemy we gift/share/and consume.
Chocolate.
   Thanks, cocoa pod.

Great Boudicca's Chariot In Yarmouth

Dawn French (*my sister*) was just 16
When we holidayed in GREAT Yarmouth.
She was home alone – not, with Great Auntie.
Best holiday ever, on the Council site,
Opposite the funfair for two weeks.
(Pocket money spent on day one).

Towed in by the RAC – sat up front –
Having broken down on the Acle Strait
(The poet in me gazing at sky and clouds,
Dad swearing and gesturing until they stopped).

A pack of Alsatians in the next tent
- We loved them all-
So, a fortnight later, motorbike repaired,
Dad thanking the gods on releasing his chariot home.
Boudicca-rich, we got back before school started.
I loudly proclaimed happy news
(Aged 9) – *I'm an Auntie.*

Family tales lived on for years,
At my mispronunciation of facts:
The offending engine part on the mantelpiece,
Truly 'Pissed-On'.

And The Old Shall Be Young *(Palindrome/Pantoum)*

In time though years have passed for flowers foiling,
He's aged no greater than he had before,
Like last summers' faded hours, gravest, spoiling
That face and image few would now adore.

He's aged no greater than he had. Before:
Complexioned youthful spots and rosy lips.
That face and image few would now adore,
Fourteen-age angst, frowns, temper; angel-sips,

Complexioned youthful spots and rosy lips.
By stardust, fire, gold hair and wing-beat heart,
For teenage angst/frowns/temper, angel-sips,
Floored flight-fall's flaxen sunshine stormed apart.

By stardust, fire, gold hair and wing-beat heart
Flawed flight-fall's flaxen sunshine stormed apart.
I wait for him to ghost me... now I'm patient.
Forever young, that mind. His body's ancient.

*

Forever young, that mind, his body's ancient;
I wait for him to ghost me now, I'm patient.
Floored flight-fall's flaxen sunshine stormed apart
By stardust, fire, gold hair and wing-beat heart.

Flawed flight-fall's flaxen sunshine stormed apart,
For teenage angst/frowns/temper. Angel-sips

(cont.)

By stardust, fire, gold hair and wing-beat heart,
Complexioned youthful spots and rosy lips.

Four teenage angst/frowns/temper/angel-sips
That face and image: few would now adore
Complexioned youthful spots and rosy lips?
He's aged no greater than he had; before. . .

That face and image, few would. Now adore:
Like last summers' faded hours' gravest spoiling.
He's aged no greater than he had before,
In time though years have passed for flowers foiling.

Impossible Silence

Drink may whisper like St Paul's,
Until I hear nothing but its dong
And still I cannot ask still; still
What you blocked my asking
       Once, and twice, and three times.
More questions? No answers.
How long do you want me silent?
       Ask? Please ask. . .
       Mixed messages of blame, of moments, speaking.
I may not have the answers.
       Want to know…
If parenting is possible; support.
Wiser than your years. An infant, grouching,
So, tell me what you want me…
       To do; to ask.

Walled Garden *(Triolet)*

The peacefulness of morning's here;
Ducks sunbathe, beak tucked into wing.
Fresh petals burst forth, bees appear,
The peacefulness of morning's here.
Can earth bloom sweet: without its sting?
Can spikes and tendrils climb or spear?
The peacefulness of morning's here,
Fresh petals burst forth, bees appear.

Rejoice, And Weep *(Triolet)*

We pay the price, a hostage comes back home,
The political climate is changing.
They zoom and clap, negotiate and roam;
We pay the price, a hostage comes back home.

Distraction salves the pain of blood-soaked loam.
Pray for Peace. The world is rearranging,
We pay the price, a hostage comes back home.
The political climate is changing.

Platinum Jubilee

So who remembers
Coronation Day? King George?
Beauty, sparkle, youthfulness…

You do? The world's changed.
And what to tell the future?
Upheavals; War; Peace.

Britannia steers home:
Let's all party anyway,
For a day. No news.

Weathered Romance *(Triolet)*

September is the cruellest month to wait
Beneficence of summer in few days.
I will pour chilled prosecco, stay out late,
September is the cruellest month to wait.

I'm wrapped in lots of woollies with my mate:
Romance is dead in – oh – so many ways.
September is the cruellest month to wait
Beneficence of summer in few days.

The Blues And Yellows Of Mother's Day

Smashed the glass of Mother's Day:
No flimsy frame nor mirror.
Expendable/long-dead/unnamed
Glass trashed to ornamental hell.
No shattered curve (feminine nor fine)
From family times of long ago.
Dreamed it all, that fairytale,
The young with happy smiles and flowers,
Wobbling in with tray piled high:
Coffee cold/burnt toast/a mug
Of juice/and marmalade sticky-sublime.
Finally, a card/a giggle/hug/then off to play.
Dream on, arthritic joints, just hope for coffee,
Or kick him out to duties (clocks wound round),
A special Mother's Day (the young sleep late).

So late…my firstborn, waiting for a dove (crows
And wood pigeons, magpies) – strut your stuff
For heavenly featherdown and sparkling stars.
A blond child, laughing, would be doubly good.
Sleep on, my stillborn; none of this world's gain.
Remember? How your Grandma died too soon. . .
Grimm fairy tales (not pink nor sweet) today.
My love, my life, redeemed with tray, but later.
A simple feast; and Mamma Mia on Play.
Uncork the gin – glass to ease dull pain –
Or just see dancing daffodils; and write.

Cold Fighters *(Pantoum)*

Compassionately take away the pain,
Away from women/children, old folks too.
We hoped to see slow torture: never. Again,
Grieving every TV screen's prime view.

Away from women, children, old folks too,
The dead are left to bury city dust.
Grieving every TV screen's prime view,
Delivering worldwide outrage; trampled trust.

The dead are left to bury city dust.
Fake news bleeds arteries of social hell,
Delivering worldwide outrage, (trampled trust:
Cold fighters - born just yesterday), so well.

Fake news bleeds arteries of social hell;
Every film shot beneath the sun's last shade,
Cold fighters, born just yesterday so well.
None counts the day nor hour life's unmade.

Every film shot beneath the sun's last shade,
Like seasons: rotten fruit will one day fall.
None counts the day nor hour life's unmade,
So breathe day into dance. What lord will call?

Like seasons, rotten fruit will one day fall.
We hoped to sea-slow torture never again.
So breathe, lord, day to dance. What will you call. . .
Compassionately take away the pain.

Make Marmalade, Not War *(Star Davidian)*

So waking stirs howled memories of hell,
Taken back from our TV screens last night.
Arising, quoting Julian's dreams so well,
Recalling blue and yellow blooms to sight.
Seasons of flags wavering.

Still heroic faces haunt in newsprint,
Telling social media posts freak silence.
Armoured ranks of nowhere roads; each footprint
Remains, as trampled hearts' intolerance.
Seasons of flowers falling.

Shooting stars of heroes cloud dull earth-dust,
Tanked up dictator's dug his mausoleum.
A man, a Jew, a family sparks heart-trust.
Remember Paddington Bear's memoriam:
Spreading marmalade; not War.

Collection Of Senryu

Pensioners, easy,
Stride into the utter east;
Find heaven, or hell

Heat from the steelworks,
As the brave live, show mettle;
Rising beyond death

Explosion on board.
Accidental munitions...
That was some bright spark

'Please take them with you,
I have no use for them now.'
Young father, to Press.

'We all have to die,
Some go to heaven; some croak.'
'Knowing our leader. . . '

Joan

She's gone. They loved her. She was special to them all,
As eulogy took quite some time to form.
The words vanished in the ceiling of my poor ears;
She's there – in flesh alone – where minds conform.

No Upwords moments mark the passage of friendship,
She's gone in all but fire and wood and ink.
The bloom of flowers, white with grief, could tremble:
She's lived more than Her Majesty can think.

So lay to rest the joy of connected moments,
Each photograph an icon of the past.
It's finished, the future's door now widely opens:
Those treasured hearts and minds hoard dreams so vast. . .

So dress well/smile a 100 contented dreams;
Stay positive with everything life seems.

(Published in Crystal Magazine, May 2022)

Gardening At 4AM *(Pantoum)*

It's the middle of the night: pain prevents sleep,
So – a gardener – I will wander, late, outside.
At 4am, there are few plants I need to keep
In check: prune/water/deadhead/or divide.

So, a gardener I will wander (late, outside),
Comforted by plants, and in love with trees.
In check/prune/water/deadhead, or divide;
Attention to that lady (cold), and, please…

Comforted by plants, and in love with trees.
'I didn't want to speak, in case you jump…'
Attention to that lady – cold and, please…
'What are you doing? Earth/out here/this clump…'

'I didn't want to speak in case you jump.
'My husband was rushed into intensive care…,'
'What are you doing… Earth! Out here, this clump…'
'It seems he has C19.' (What's that?) *'I can't wait there.*

'My husband was rushed into intensive care.'
'You must be worried sick!' This old lady sits.
'It seems he has C19, what's that? I can't wait there,
In isolation here, hot chocolate, tips…'

'You must be worried sick!' This old lady sits…
Swapping gardening hints with schoolgirl giggles.
'In isolation here, hot chocolate/tips.
Until daylight/peaceful good mornings/respective wiggles.

(cont.)

Swapping gardening hints, with schoolgirl giggles.
Gardens heal (sleepful, to our respective beds),
Until daylight, peaceful good mornings. Respective wiggles:
It's time for bed (till 1pm, without meds).

Gardens heal, sleepful to our respective beds,
At 4am there are few plants I need to keep.
It's time for bed – till 1pm – without meds.
It's the middle of the night; pain prevents sleep. . .

(Published in Reach Poetry, April 2022)

Friendly Heaven From Seasons Past *(Davidian)*

I could imagine a heaven like that:
Like wave on rosy wave of trumpet clouds;
Sun's sheen so bright, no mediocre shades.
A raucous, lurid rhododendron spring,
The past and future blending.

I could imagine a heaven like that –
Like a mist springing from manicured lawn
And daisies never out of place among
A bluebell sea, for ever England's shore.
The past and future blending.

I could imagine a heaven like that;
Like wisteria's azure - arbour's surf -
A bench secluded from earth's harshest stare.
No queues of tourists for a photograph;
The past and future blending.

I could imagine a heaven like that,
Like trees of proud magnolias in bloom
And late daffodils virgin as the snow
And buttercups that drop like clotted cream,
The past and future blending.

I could imagine a heaven like that.
Like chinks of classic crockery piled high
And pots of creamy tea and buttered scones.
Friends' smiles, as fairy cups, when we get home -
The past and future blending.

(cont.)

I could imagine a heaven like that,
When Norfolk's Blickling Hall may fail to charm
And loved ones wait, but on some distant shore
Where life is spring's eternal psalmody,
The past and future's blending.

(Published in Rubies in the Darkness)

Frozen Winter

It is all water now
                     And how my poetry flaws
To flood the earth.
Not visible, except in sodden ground
And foliage budding, blooming every day.

It's winter now
                     And all I see is how the poetry flows
To drought my store of fuel and feed and darkness.
There's nothing left within this barn:
                     The doors are opened wide
On heaven/earth and sea/sky/storm.

It's scarlet-frozen Frost's cruel feeling earth,
Dull corm that's fat with sap, potential stoppered.
Uncork my hopefulness like rocket spark,
To fill remembrance skies with what has been.

One day, when ice-crust melts
                     And my sun shines,
Oh, then you'll see their avenue of trees
In topiary of what has gone before.
Then, and only then,
                     You will see my daughter.

(Published in Littoral Magazine/Spring Solstice 2022)

Bob

It's 70 years since you were first an infant,
Born with your mother's genes; your grandsire's too.
So did it limit your capacity?
Or life's experience that none can choose?

It's 70 years since you were not called Stephen;
No feast of celebration – pint of Shippoes.
A boy is joy enough though, don't you think?
A choice of music/footpaths/lives to choose?

It's 70 years of boats/bikes/combos/camping/
School/home/jobs/career/and family time.
Meticulously detailed, memory's trace,
Young ears enough to listen; not to learn.

It's 70 years you cannot live again,
Filled with worthwhile pursuits: in(sight) or sound.
So who is blind, or sees? For life is rich.
So have your cake, and eat it. Celebrate.

The Journey

The funeral, you might say, was satisfactory:
The midwife delivering a pre-deceased premature history,
Prescient with demise.
This was easy for her: a full/complete life,
Relatives/friends moist-eyed
                                        In all the right places.
Packed hall, post-Lockdown, and hymns;
Oh yes, singing.
The daughter beautiful, the son intelligent . . .
(The son brave, the daughter intelligent).

IF you can sound last hours, let love show,
With every mourner grieving their own loss . . .
Then nothing of your self will be forgotten;
And bravely I will be a man, *my son.*
A hard time I had of it - the journey -
Set down in my native county,
The hotel/restaurant full of foreign
Phrases/wine/no dancing.

The wake bled chandeliers' tears/a bar queue,
And distractions from bier and depth.
The poet in me dies with fewer mourners,
A grave that's hidden on some distant moor.
Or, I pray, tucked in beside my firstborn;
love of my life following late (aged 95). . .
when all my qualities have been long-
                                        forgotten.

(Published in Crystal Magazine, March 2022)

The King

I have a dream,
That banners will wave bright with joy and peace,
That songs will sing and children play, as one,
That marches laugh and whistle, light with fun.
I have a dream.

I have a dream,
That cheering crowds will hold a neighbour's hand,
That community halls will open everywhere,
That shouts/applause will encourage all to vote.
I have a dream.

I have a dream,
That firework sparkle dances full of hope,
That smiles behind late masks will be revealed,
That thanksgiving meals include a stranger/friend.
I have a dream.

I have a dream,
That leaders will show presidential charm,
That grace/humility/acceptance lives,
That hateful rhetoric and mob-rule dies.
I have a dream.

(Published in Reach Poetry, March 2021)

Silent Night *(Pantoum)*

Dull foreign hordes of aliens, so unmanned,
Deep gazing on the starry host of heaven.
A silent bidin' night is all we planned,
best mates around the fire/good wine/unleaven-

Deep gazing on the starry host of heaven,
Such natal star to tempt soft robes to pack.
Best mates around the fire, good wine, unleaven-
Delilahs dancing dark fires from our back.

Such natal star to tempt soft robes to pack,
Precious female cargo gorged by grace.
Delilahs dancing dark fires from our back.
My ass aches, trumps the timing force of race.

Precious female cargo gauged by grace.
No place. This inn's full/locked/the robbing night…
My ass aches, trumps the timing! Force of 'r. Ace!
A boy! At home. Stone cradle! Towels! And, light!!

No place. This inn's full/locked/the robbing night.
Please, let us in! A lamb. Wild angel cries…
A boy at home. Stone cradle towelled and light.
God! Gold is better! Ugh!! Gift lullabies.

Please let us in. A lamb! Wild angel cries.
A silent bidin' night is all we planned.
God… Gold (is better). Myrrh – gift lullabies.
Dull foreign hordes of aliens so unmanned.

Stars Shine On *(Star Shine in Lockdown)*

So
Three
Ancient gifts
Remain, in cloud-wings
Softly descending silently upon
Hearts and homes worldwide, mourning
Infinite noise of travel-strains; for we are beached
Natally, in that cave where all we hold dear remains, pausing:
Enlightening home, if minds sustain Glorias
In excelsis.   SHINE on, as home,
Never leaving that stable
Lofty-high bleat
Of lambs/calves.
Christmas
Kindling
Dawning
Orbs of
White
Noel.

(Published in Star Tips, December 2020)

And You, My Father

Morning as broken as the shivers of my art,
Squirming too early, too sleep-lost when the rain comes.
Blackbird has soaken my bright canvas with dull worms,
Parting dull tunnels of earth tracks gouged to airspace.

Squirming too early, too sleep-lost when the rain comes,
Nightmare and absence; dark phantoms draped in dreamscape.
Parting dull tunnels of earth tracks gouged to airspace,
Screaming for plastics discarded until the call.

Nightmare and absence, dark phantoms draped in dreamscape,
Hums loudly; my father, a hover without wings.
Screaming for plastics discarded until the call:
Earpierce – not air peace – wrung loudly into silence.

Hums loudly – my father – a hover without wings,
Stringing brash sunset at his ending and my start.
Ear-pieced, not air-pierced, wrung loudly into silence;
Acquiescence of the butterfly left cold now.

Stringing brash sunset at his ending and my start,
blackbird has soaken my bright canvas with dull worms.
Acquiescence of the butterfly left cold now:
Morning as broken as the shivers of my art.

(Published in Star Tips, September 2019)

68

The Spinster's Prayer Revisited

Dear Spinster, I know
You want it all now.
My best andropod
From Cupid, and how
He's got to have everything
Dashing and fine.
A perfection of Adonis,
And in his prime.

I know you have waited
Too long – so not fair –
So here is my promise:
It was once all there.
I had him lined up
To answer your need.
A spectacular specimen:
Perfection indeed.

However, while he prayed for you…
Not your hobbies,
He whiled away lonely hours
With causes and lobbies.
Inventive, gold-hearted,
One of a kind;
Though radically altered,
I hope you don't mind.

So now, as you wanted,
Rough corners snipped off,
Keep him (creatively):   *(cont.)*

Survival's a laugh.
Olympic eyes/teeth
And ready to get laid.
Name changed to Adoné:
She's virtually handmade.

(Published in Quantum Leap, February 2019)

David

David Norris-Kay: David was christened David Austin in 1949, and adopted his writing name with the encouragement of his friend and fellow poet the late Margaret Munro-Gibson (Margaret Hoole) who wrote under her Grandmother's and Mother's maiden names. David now does the same. He started writing poetry in 1967, inspired by Simon and Garfunkel's lyrics. His poetry is lyrical and a lot of it is written in traditional forms, although he also writes in free verse. His free verse poem, 'Butterfly' won first prize in the Salopian Poetry Society's competition in 1981, and his poem 'Autumn's Reflection' won the third prize of £250 in Forward Poetry's competition in 2004. David is divorced and lives happily on his own in Sheffield, Yorkshire, England. He is inspired by his happy 1950s childhood, the natural world, (Especially The Peak District National Park) and his friend's children. He writes mostly poetry, although his 4000 word, supernatural short story 'The Moss Garden' was published twice in 'Monomyth' magazine (Atlantean Publishing) in 1986, and again in 2020. His poetry is widely published in the United Kingdom, Australia, The USA and India. His work has appeared in The National Poetry Anthology and 'Heart Shoots' (IDP) in aid of the Macmillan Cancer Charity. David's 83 page poetry collection 'From Time-Buried Years' (Indigo Dreams Publishing) is available from him for £10 (inc p&p) by emailing davidnorriskay@ymail.com PayPal accepted. He is a member of the ALCS and The Society of Authors.

Wendy

Wendy Webb: Born in the Midlands, Wendy found home and family life in Norfolk. She edited Star Tips poetry magazine 2001-2021. Published in various small press magazines (Reach, Quantum Leap, Crystal, Envoi, Seventh Quarry), she was placed First in Writing Magazine's pantoum poetry competition. She enjoyed devising new poetry forms (Davidian, Magi, etc). She wrote her father's biography, 'Bevin Boy', shortly before his death. Then she wrote her own autobiography (as a poet). She has read extensively from Chaucer to modern-day poets, inspired to attempt many traditional forms and free verse. Favourite poets (in no particular order): Dylan Thomas, Gerard Manley Hopkins, Sophie Hannah, John Burnside, John Betjeman, the Romantic Poets (especially Wordsworth), George Herbert, William Blake, Emily Dickinson, Mary Webb, Norman Bissett, William Shakespeare, the Bible, and the Rubaiyat of Omar Khayyam. Oh, and Bob Dylan, James Blunt, Leonard Cohen, and Katie Melua. Recently, she has tried a number of online outlets for her work (including Littoral Magazine, Lothlorien and Meek Colin) and has enjoyed the challenges through Autumn Voices. She's a keen gardener; and rides an electric trike. With dodgy knees, and dodgy hearing, isn't life fun?

Acknowledgements

David -
'Old ones, new ones, loved ones, neglected ones' -
Alberto Semprini

Butterfly, Dragonflies, Lorraine aged 8 and Autumn's Reflection are included in David's collection,
'From Time-Buried Years'. (Indigo Dreams Publishing)

Some of these poems were published in 'Reach Poetry'. 'Salopeot' (The magazine of the Salopian Poetry Society.) 'Star Tips For Writers' and 'Bard' (Atlantean Publishing)

I would like to thank all the editors who published my work, especially Ronnie Goodyer (Indigo Dreams Publishing) Roger Hoult (The Salopian Poetry Society) , D.J. Tyrer (Atlantean Publishing) Wendy Webb (Norfolk Writers) Meek, (Inherit The Earth Publications) Peter Pike (Australia) and Dr H Tulsi (India)

Wendy –
For the many poetry magazines (and editors) that have flowered and fallen. For the brave and stalwart editors of Reach, Sarasvati, Quantum Leap, Crystal, and others, and for the rising online stars (Littoral, Lothlorien, Meek, Autumn Voices).

Publisher.

inherit_theearth@btbtinternet.com